From Concept
To
Community

**How I Built An Online Community
And Took It Viral In 25 Days
With Little Money And No SEO**

By
April L. Hamilton

Dedicated to the early content contributors and
registered members at Publetariat.com: the
site's success has much less to do with me, the
founder, than it does with YOU, the community.

- April L. Hamilton

Table of Contents

1. <u>Introduction</u>

This year, at the O'Reilly Tools of Change conference in Manhattan, the buzzword of the event was *community*. From the beginning of the conference to the end, from the keynote speeches to the breakout sessions, from the tutorials to the lunchtime small talk, online community-building was the preoccupation du jour.

Publishers and authors were exhorted to focus at least as much attention on building online communities around their content as on creating the content itself. Luminary thinkers like Jeff Jarvis of Buzzmachine and Tim O'Reilly of O'Reilly Media assured us that the very survival of our businesses may well depend on our ability to form and grow vibrant, interactive, online communities around our content.

1.1. <u>The "Why" Of Community-Building</u>

Thanks to the phenomenon of web content created *by* users, *for* users, such as blogging, YouTube, comment forms attached to online articles, citizen journalism via Twitter and personal websites, today's media consumer is no longer willing to accept a one-way infodump from authors and publishers. Media consumers have come to expect a genuine, two-way conversation, and more importantly, have come to realize that their side of that conversation can be just as important and influential to the general public as that of an author or publisher.

This is the "why" of community-building, which came through loud and clear to conference attendees. We returned to our offices feeling highly motivated to begin, or strengthen, our own community-building initiatives, but had been given very little to work with in the way of "how". That's where this little book comes in.

1.2. <u>My Own Community-Building Story</u>

As it happens, I'd spent the weeks leading up to the conference creating Publetariat, a new online community of my own, and announced the official launch of that community at the conference, on February 11, 2009.

One week later, on February 17, 2009, I ran my new community's website address through websitegrader, a web-based engine which calculates and rates the influence and reach of websites based on site traffic, Search Engine Optimization (SEO) factors, the site's Rich Site Summary (RSS) feed traffic, and more.

Within Publetariat's report, I found the following, startling statistic:

E. Traffic Rank: Top 6.92 %

Alexa is an online service that measures traffic for millions of sites on the Internet in a similar way to Nielsen television show ratings.

Your website has an Alexa rank of **2,125,265** which is in the top **6.92 %** of all websites.

According to the report, in just seven days, Publetariat traffic had climbed into the top 6.92% of all websites all over the world. I knew the site had been doing well in its first week, but this didn't seem possible.

I checked the traffic statistics on the site's web server and found that on 2/17 alone, the overall site had indeed received 9,046 hits, and the site's RSS feed had received over 1,200 hits.

To verify these results further, I went to the Alexa site and punched Publetariat into their traffic ranking search box. While the site was nowhere near popular enough to rate in the top 100,000 sites worldwide, I discovered that site traffic for the month to date tallied the site's rank up to an amazing 727,638:

Traffic Rank for Publetariat.com: ⑦

Alexa traffic rank based on a combined measure of page views and users (reach)

Yesterday	1 wk. Avg.	3 mos. Avg.	3 mos. Change
N/A*	727,638	2,214,826	--

Furthermore, I discovered that when websitegrader.com calculated its overall traffic ranking of the top 6.92% for Publetariat, it had done so based on Alexa's 3-month average of traffic.

Taking into account the fact that Publetariat had only been launched one week before the report was run, I decided to recalculate the site's traffic average for just one month: February—the one month during which Publetariat had been open to the public.

To my astonishment, I found that Publetariat traffic ranked in the top 2% of all websites worldwide for the month of February, 2009—this, with the site open to the public for just one week, the month only half over, and traffic still growing.

What makes these results even more astonishing still is the fact that I'd only come up with the *idea* for Publetariat.com one month before, on January 15, 2009. I registered the domain on January 16, but didn't begin development of the site in earnest until January 24.

In just 18 days, I'd taken the site from concept to go-live. In just 25 days, I'd taken it from concept to a traffic rating in the top 2% of all websites!

And I did it with no budget to speak of, little prior experience in community-building, and a non-expert development staff of one: me.

1.3. <u>SEO—Or Lack Thereof</u>

An interesting aspect of that websitegrader report is the fact that Publetariat failed pretty miserably on most of its Search Engine Optimization (SEO) -based metrics, causing the site's overall "grade" to come in at just 71/100. Yet Publetariat still managed to draw enough traffic to get into the top 2% of all websites in its first week, and site traffic and membership rolls have continued to grow despite the site's total lack of consideration for SEO.

Given that the goal of SEO is to increase site traffic, and my site traffic has been high from the outset, I'd have to say I don't regret giving SEO short shrift. I may eventually get around to adding some tags and metadata to my pages, but I have no plans to concentrate any significant effort on SEO on Publetariat going forward.

Publetariat also received low marks from websitegrader in terms of 'Social Mediasphere', because it had no "Diggs" and only 8 de.licio.us bookmarks, and in the

'Blogosphere' area, because it had not been ranked on Technorati's blog directory service. None of this seems to have had a negative impact on site traffic, which leads me to believe a lot of the time, money and energies people are pouring into courting Diggs and other social bookmarking notices is time, money and energies wasted—or at least, better spent elsewhere.

As it turns out, if you view your site building and launch process as a community-building effort in its own right, by the time you're ready to take your site live, you'll have a small army of grassroots cheerleaders and publicists ready to go to bat for you.

1.4. <u>What's In This Little Book</u>

In this little book, I will lay out the process and strategies I employed to build, launch and promote Publetariat. And if you're wondering how such a small book can possibly provide all the information you need to start your own successful, online community, the answer is this: community-building doesn't have to be as complicated or difficult as you've probably been led to believe. The keys to success are:

- Concept

- Branding

- Time Your Launch

- Recruit Allies

- Use A Content Management System

- Community-Friendly Development

- A Staged Release

- Keep The Momentum Going

There is also a chapter on Monetization. Monetization isn't really a key to community-building success so much as a necessary evil of community-building. In my Monetization chapter, I explain how to approach it in a way that will make it more palatable to your community.

2. Concept

All successful online communities have one thing in common: they fulfill a public need or desire. They inform, entertain, or improve the site visitor's life in a way that's meaningful enough to keep that visitor coming back.

As a strong advocate for indie authors and small imprints, I've long been aware of the need for an online community dedicated to that audience. There are countless online sites, blogs and discussion groups for writers, but before I launched my community, Publetariat, there was no single site, blog or discussion group in existence to address all the needs and concerns of this specific demographic.

In the case of the community you hope to build, you may not have the luxury of being able to identify a need and fulfill it, as I did. You may have been issued an order to build your community around a specific book, imprint, author, product or company. You may need to build a community around yourself or your own work.

In such a situation, you must identify your target audience for the community, then identify what that audience will find useful, interesting, entertaining, informative or otherwise desirable about the thing or person around which/whom you'll be building your community.

2.1. <u>Your Product Versus Your Community</u>

Brainstorm two lists of traits: one list to describe your intended audience, and another to describe the thing or person around which you'll be building your community. Don't worry about trying to make them align or intersect at this point, just treat the lists as entirely independent of one another. Also, don't try to be too specific at this stage of the game; work with generalities.

Consider a mainstream imprint that publishes Young Adult romances with supernatural elements.

Imprint Traits:

1. Subsidiary of large, trusted publisher

2. Feminine branding

3. Edgy cover design

4. Small catalog of titles

5. Youthful authors

6. Forward-thinking, techno-savvy staff

Intended Audience Traits:

1. Female

2. Teenaged

3. Love music, clothes, technology

4. Desire popularity, exclusivity

5. View selves as sophisticated young women

6. Strong readers

7. Highly computer-literate

Note that the two lists do not have to contain a matching number of items.

Now look at your two lists together, side by side, and see where the traits of the first list can speak to the traits of your intended audience, on the second list. In the example at hand, there are numerous intersections.

The imprint is a subsidiary of a well-known publisher and maintains a small catalog of titles; these traits speak to the audience's desire for exclusivity. The imprint employs edgy cover designs and signs youthful authors; these traits speak to the audience's age and desire to be seen as sophisticated. The imprint's techno-savvy staff aligns well with the needs of a highly computer-literate and technology-obsessed youth culture. And of course, the feminine branding aligns perfectly with the predominant gender of the intended audience.

But what if the thing around which you're building a community isn't so concrete? What if it's more of a philosophy, such as was the case for Publetariat? You really only need to construct one list. Since your intended audience is a group that already subscribes to the philosophy at the heart of your intended community, the list that describes the philosophy also describes the intended audience. Examples of this type of community are sites focused on eco-awareness, social change, or religion.

Hang on to your lists, because you'll be using them in the branding, design, construction and promotion of your community.

3. **Branding**

The next stage in the process is branding: coming up with a name and aesthetic identity for your community. This is where many, if not most, corporate-backed community-building initiatives fail, because the tendency is to simply name and brand the site the same as the specific thing around which the community is being built—typically, the name of a company or product line.

That approach makes a lot of sense for an informational site aimed at consumers, because a consumer will very likely type the name of the product or company directly into her browser when searching for more information or technical support. However, an informational site is *not* a community.

3.1. **A Community Is A Community**

At this stage you need to forget about corporate or personal identity and think about your intended, online community the same way you think of "real world" communities, such as neighborhoods, towns and clubs.

13

An effective and successful community is one to which people want to belong, and in which people feel special and distinct from the population at large. Its members share a sense of pride in the community, as well as loyalty and even protectiveness toward that community.

Corporations and big, commercial brand names don't tend to inspire any feelings of belonging, specialness, loyalty or protectiveness, because by their very nature, corporations are faceless and impersonal, with a revolving door of executives and product lines, and a profit motive as their primary reason for being.

Back in the day, Apple was a brand its customers wore like a badge of honor. As the company has grown increasingly large, rich and impersonal, its early culture of 'computer as object of affection' has given way to a culture of 'gadget as object of hip affluence'.

Apple's customers may still be every bit as loyal to its product lines as ever, but they no longer feel that same, early sense of community that once seemed inherent in the formerly underdog company. Rather, they form their own communities based on their specific interests in Apple's various product lines: theiphoneblog.com, ilounge.com, and ipodlinux.com, to name a few.

Look back at the trait list you brainstormed for your intended community. Imagine that group as real human beings standing in a crowd right in front of you, and further, imagine that crowd forming a "real world" club. What would they want their club to be like? What image would they want their club to convey? What functions or features would they look to the club to provide? Once you've got a clear mental picture of the club your community wants, it's time to come up with a name.

3.2. Naming Your Site

There are two schools of thought when it comes to website naming: literal and explicit (i.e., freecreditreport.com, newsweek.com) versus evocative and ambiguous (i.e., twitter.com, mashable.com).

The draw of a literal and explicit website name, such as www.lowcostinsurance.com, is the high likelihood that web surfers will come across the URL via a simple search or even by typing the site name directly into a web browser. The downside of this option is that the name isn't particularly memorable or appealing. If a site visitor doesn't happen to bookmark the site, in trying to find it later on he may type in variants such as lowpriceinsurance.com, goodpriceinsurance.com, or similar. He may remember the idea behind the name, but isn't likely to remember the name itself.

An evocative and ambiguous website name can be much more memorable and appealing, but isn't as likely to be found accidentally by web surfers. On the other hand, an effective name of this type tends to really stick in one's consciousness and incite curiosity.

In general, if you're hoping to establish a brand that defines or references a culture, philosophy or lifestyle, evocative and ambiguous is the way to go. Given that online communities generally define or reference a culture, philosophy or lifestyle, it's no surprise that the most successful online communities tend to have evocative and ambiguous names. Consider BoingBoing, Zwinky and Buzznet, for example.

You may be thinking of MySpace and Facebook as prime exceptions, since their names are literal and fairly explicit. However, MySpace and Facebook are not actually online communities. Rather, they're platforms upon which their members can build their own online communities.

I can't tell you exactly what to name your community, but I can tell you how I came up with the name for

Publetariat. I began by focusing on the fact that the primary distinguishing characteristic of my audience was independence. I toyed with many names featuring the word "indie" in various forms, but none struck me as The One.

Digging a bit deeper, I thought about the way this group of writers and small publishers feel excluded or even alienated from the mainstream, and realized this is the crux of their sense of kinship with one another. Where the mainstream is dominated by faceless corporations that publish, my audience is a group of *people* who publish.

Once I started thinking of that group as comprised of the common man, it wasn't much of a leap to the word "proletariat", and from there, to "Publetariat". All I had left to do was verify that the name was not already taken. I began by Googling the name, to ensure no companies or products were using the name. When my search returned no results, I looked up publetariat.com on networksolutions.com, and finding the domain available, I promptly registered it.

Note: I registered the domain for five years, which is supposedly more SEO–friendly than registering for just one year at a time. However, I didn't do this for SEO purposes. Frankly, I'm the sort of person who doesn't like to have things hanging over my head and registering for five years means I don't have to think about it again for four years. Network Solutions also provides discounts for longer-term registrations. I maintain several websites, and even though I've always registered them for longer than one year, in my experience, doing so has not been a significant traffic driver.

3.3. **The Aesthetic Of Your Site**

You'll find that your mental picture of the real world version of your community, together with your choice of name, will naturally guide the aesthetic look of the site. In the case of Publetariat, it was a no-brainer to go with a tongue-in-cheek take on communist propaganda. Likewise, it's obvious why Twitter's emblem is a bird.

If no symbols or images come to mind in association with your chosen name, think about the commonalities, desires and motivations of your intended audience. The goal at this point isn't to map out the design of an entire website, but to come up with a unifying aesthetic theme, or general look, for the site. Imagine the kind of look you might come up with for the site if it were a print magazine instead of an online community.

3.4. <u>A Mission Or Motto</u>

The last step in branding your site is coming up with a mission statement, or motto. Let your notions of what your audience will want to get out of the site guide your thought process here, and avoid anything that sounds even remotely like marketing-speak.   The mission statement or motto should reflect your audience's sensibilities and reason for belonging to the community, *not* your company's advertising message.

For example, given the Young Adult, supernatural romance reader community discussed previously, "Girls who love [Imprint Name] books" is a much less desirable motto than, "Books That Bite," or "The only thing to fear is boring books," for example.

Notice how the latter examples play to the audience's desire to appear sophisticated, as well as their interest in stories with supernatural elements; there's nothing cutesy, ad-like, or patronizing there.

4. **Plan Your Launch**

You've barely registered your site's name, but it's already time to start thinking about your eventual launch.

4.1. **Find An Event**

Do some research to identify upcoming large, public events at which the intended audience for your community is likely to be out in force. Look for conventions, conferences, media events, concerts, sporting events, trade shows, large social gatherings—any big, public event which is right up your intended audience's alley.

Barring that, shoot for an event where attendees relate to the intended audience of your community in some way. For example, if your community is aimed at school teachers but you can't locate any upcoming big events for teachers, look for events where parents will be in attendance with their school-age children. Alternatively, you could seek out events thrown for school administrators. Many of those event attendees will pass the word along to teachers they know.

Returning to the example of the community for teen girls who read supernatural romances—and notice how I'm framing statements about the community around the girls, *not* the imprint—, you can try concerts featuring the artists who are most popular with teen girls.

Ideally, quite a few people at the event will be influential members of your intended audience, and at least some will be members of the mainstream media.

4.2. <u>Plan For The Announcement</u>

Your announcement doesn't have to take place onstage at the event. It can take the form of posters and handouts with the site name and URL on them. The handouts can be as modest as a postcard, or they can be small premiums with the site name and URL printed on them, such as pens, keychains, stickers, temporary tattoos, glow sticks, or anything else that will appeal to your intended audience.

If you're going to hand out premium items, just make sure they aren't against the rules of the venue where the event is taking place (i.e., don't give away flying discs at a concert venue).

An even more low-key and low-budget approach that can still be very effective is to attend the event right alongside your intended audience, talk up your site and hand out business cards to everyone you meet; print up the cards with the site name and URL on one side and a brief description of the community on the other.

You'll learn more about how to maximize the effectiveness of your Go-Live announcement in the A Staged Release chapter, but you'll need to set the date for that final launch, and if applicable, prepare or order your handouts, early on.

5. Recruit Allies

You've got a name, an aesthetic sense of what you want your site to look like, and an idea of your site's motto or mission statement. Before you start building the site, you need to begin your efforts to recruit some allies.

Beginning the recruitment effort before you begin to build the site allows you to field responses and send out more requests for help or input as needed while you work on site development. If you build first, then recruit, your go-live date will be delayed for as long as it takes you to line up your allies. Even more importantly, recruiting allies early on ensures a renewable stream of site content, as well as facilitating a staged marketing approach and a staged site release, as you'll see later in this book.

5.1. Why Recruit Allies?

Even if you already have a full staff assigned to your community-building initiative, you need to recruit allies who can lend your new community authority and credibility in the eyes of the site's audience, while also extending the reach of your future promotional efforts.

Corporate voices, like those on your staff, will be viewed with some degree of suspicion by the community. After all, if they're on the company payroll, doesn't that make them company men and women? You need to get some trusted (and trustworthy) outsiders involved. Your allies will be your most powerful resources in getting your site to go viral as well.

So, who are these allies? There are two primary types: Contributors and Influencers.

5.2. <u>Contributors</u>

Contributors are people you will invite to contribute content (i.e., articles) to your community. Seek out individuals who would probably be in the audience for your site, and already have a certain amount of stature with respect to the subject or mission of your site in the eyes of other likely community members. Look for bloggers with significant site traffic, and subject-area experts with a quality list of writing credits or an impressive web presence.

For example, if your community will center on classic cars, you'd want to reach out to classic car enthusiast bloggers, authors of popular relevant articles on Squidoo, eHow, etc., authors who regularly contribute to car-centric magazines and websites, and other online voices of passion and expertise about classic cars.

5.3. **Influencers**

There are two types of Influencers. The first group consists of people who are already running popular blogs or websites about the topic or product around which your community will be centered, but aren't primarily strong writers. The second group also run popular sites or blogs, but on topics not directly related to your site that are still of great interest to your audience.

If you're building a community around a computer programming book series for example, the first type of Influencer might have a blog with tips and tricks for the type of programming featured in your books, and the second type might run a website offering reviews of the latest techno-gadgets. The second site isn't directly related to your site's mission, but your intended audience of computer programmers is definitely interested in techno-gadgets as well.

These individuals are influential voices where your product or subject is concerned, and if you can win them over you will also win over their respective audiences.

Influencers will be recruited later on in the development process and discussed in greater detail later in this book, but as you search for Contributors, you can compile a side list of likely Influencers. In some cases, your chosen Contributors will also be Influencers.

5.4. <u>Compensating Allies</u>

You don't necessarily have to compensate your allies with money.

Occasional contributors may be satisfied with the exposure they will receive on your site as subject-area experts, the ability to promote their own sites/books/projects in a one- to two-line 'about the author' passage at the end of each article they contribute, and a Contributor profile page, in which they can further promote themselves and their work.

Regular contributors can be compensated with all the same exposure opportunities as occasional contributors, and given free advertising on your site in addition. In the case of Influencers, a straightforward ad or link exchange is typically all that's required.

6. Use A Content Management System

I built the framework of Publetariat in a matter of days, with virtually no budget and a non-expert development staff of one: me.

By 'framework' I mean everything on the site except content (i.e., articles, blog posts, community forum posts—everything that would be contributed by Contributors and site visitors). By 'matter of days' I mean less than one week. By 'virtually no budget' I mean I spent less than US$200, all in hosting fees. And by 'non-expert' I mean I had no prior experience with the development software used to build the site.

How did I do it? Through the use of a Content Management System (CMS).

6.1. Content Management Systems

A CMS is basically a toolkit you use to build websites, and a number of them are geared specifically to non-technical users. A CMS is to online community-building what Microsoft FrontPage is to static (informational,

29

non-interactive) website development: these are tools that make it very easy for non-programmers to build attractive, full-featured websites via a simple administrator interface that keeps most of the site code out of sight and mind.

Since quality, scalability (room to grow) and stability were priorities for me when building Publetariat, I was willing to invest significant money in a CMS. I researched every CMS I could find online and in email conversations with developer acquaintances, and eventually narrowed the field to just three options:

- Expression Engine (EE)

- Joomla!

- Drupal

All three options are template-based, meaning you can start with a website/web page template, much like using an MS Word template, and then customize it to suit your specific wants and needs.

All three employ plug-ins and modules (blocks of pre-written, pre-packaged code) to simplify and speed the development process.

All three provide a rich feature set, including just about any option you might want for your intended site (i.e., secure membership; multiple, privileged users can contribute content; blogging; hierarchical structure for article creation and storage; community forum module; administrator tools; etc.).

Joomla! and Drupal are both open-source, meaning the software is issued under licenses guaranteeing anybody rights to freely use, modify, and redistribute the code at no cost. Both have been developed, and are maintained and documented, on a largely volunteer basis, with some supplemental support from outside sponsors and user donations.

One common worry with any open-source solution is the future availability of that solution, but since both Joomla! and Drupal have been around for years and each is supported by a passionate community of users and volunteer developers, I don't think either one will be going away any time soon. Also, both Drupal and Joomla! are well-represented in terms of mainstream, corporate users.

Where EE has a fulltime, paid staff of developers and support personnel, both Drupal and Joomla! are mainly extended, enriched and supported by volunteer-contributed modules and documentation. Regarding development history, Joomla! just hasn't been around as long as EE or Drupal. Drupal's developer community is much larger than that of Joomla!, and as a result it has a much larger inventory of available volunteer-contributed modules and documentation.

EE is a totally commercial product, and as such there are significant licensing fees attached to the product. It can be an advantage to have a fulltime staff of paid professionals standing behind the product, constantly improving it, and providing training and support for it, but you will have to pay for that advantage.

Any of the three choices would've met my needs in terms of feature set, but in the end I chose Drupal.

While EE might've offered me more control and more flexibility with advanced administration options, it was on orders of magnitude above and beyond my needs. Moreover, with increasing control and flexibility comes increasing complexity, and I didn't want to have to read books and take classes to figure out how to take full advantage of my CMS. The final nail in EE's coffin was the price; after all, why pay a premium for CMS options I wasn't sure I really needed?

Joomla! actually edges out Drupal slightly when it comes to ease of setup and use, as well as in the design of the community forum (discussion board) area. Also, the Joomla! site itself is very well-organized and easy to navigate. However, the situation here is the opposite as that of EE: ease of use sometimes comes at the cost of advanced site configuration options.

In my case, some of those advanced options really mattered to me. For example, Drupal far exceeds Joomla's capabilities in the area of user management. While Joomla! allows you to set up a small number of secure user groups to allow privileged users access to various areas of your site which are restricted from non-privileged users (i.e., an interface for creating and publishing articles), Drupal allows many more secure groups to be created and allows you to grant or deny access to members of those groups right down to the individual field level.

Drupal also has many, many more volunteer-contributed modules and plug-ins than Joomla!, which makes it possible to add virtually any feature or widget you can imagine to your site. Everything from something as irreverent as a virtual Magic 8 Ball to something as important as integration for Google AdSense is available.

I would undoubtedly get more consistency across modules and documentation with EE, but so long as the modules and documentation provided by Drupal meet my needs, there didn't seem to be a good justification for me to spend the money on EE.

Moreover, using an open-source CMS dovetailed perfectly with the indie ethic of Publetariat.

I suggest you research the various CMS options available to you with your own specific needs in mind. Development efforts continue daily on just about any large software package you can imagine, so the information I've provided here about EE, Joomla! and Drupal may be stale-dated by the time you're reading this book.

6.2. The Process of Building The Site

The process of building Publetariat was fairly simple:

1. Download CMS software

2. Sign up & pay for hosting

3. Install CMS software on host server, using provided directions

4. Configure installation, using provided directions

5. Select a site template

6. Customize template to enable/include features I wanted, disable/exclude features I didn't

7. Set up user groups & security levels, assign rights

8. Search module list for additional, desired features, install and configure them using provided directions

9. Test

10. Upload content (articles)

Thanks to the easy administrator interface I was able to accomplish all of this in about 5 days, working on the project only part-time.

I'll admit there were a few times when I hit a snag and had to go in search of help, but between the Drupal.org online community and the many, many Drupal experts who run their own blogs and websites on the subject, I never had to wait longer than about 4 hours for an answer to my problem.

6.3. A "Coming Soon" Page

Once you've got your hosting set up and your CMS installed on the server, begin your development effort by parking a static, "coming soon" page on your server. There should be a simple mechanism provided by your CMS to redirect anyone who visits the site to the "coming soon" page, while still allowing you and anyone else on your development team to access the full development site by typing its specific address directly into your browser.

The "coming soon" page should mimic the theme/look of the community you're developing, and include some kind of teaser text describing all the wonderful and exciting features of the community to come. It should also include an email address to which interested parties can send an email in order to receive updates on the site.

The "coming soon" page is needed because you will begin promoting your new community long before it's ready for launch, and because you don't want members of the general public to see your site while it's still in development.

7. Community-Friendly Development

As you work with your chosen CMS to develop your site, enabling and disabling various features, configuring site details and so on, always keep your goal of community-building uppermost in mind.

7.1. Make Your Users Feel At Home

In essence, you are building an online "home" for your users. Make it a welcoming and empowering place.

If you want users to truly feel a part of your community and become cheerleaders for your site, allow each one to customize and extend his little section of the site to the degree that's possible without compromising your site's security or mission.

Give him the tools and features that will enable him to feel *at home* in *your home*. For example, give him:

- a member profile page where he can share information about himself and his sites

- the ability to upload a custom user avatar (picture)

- other customization options, such as the ability to set preferences for site colors and content display upon user login

- the ability to re-sort discussion threads according to his own preferences

- control over his own content: if he posts a blog entry, discussion board entry or poll, he should be allowed to edit or delete it himself

- the option to provide as much or as little information in his member profile as he wishes – keep required fields to a minimum

- the ability to register for membership with an absolute minimum of required information—if at all possible, limit required registration information to a username, password and a valid email address

This last bullet point may seem counterintuitive if one of your major goals in member registration is to accumulate demographic data for future marketing campaigns, but job one for that future campaign is accumulating enough members to make the campaign worthwhile.

Make it as hassle-free as possible to join. The more frequently newly-registered members visit the site, the more quickly they will begin to feel comfortable enough to provide more information about themselves.

Allow your site members to indulge in some self-promotion on your site. After all, communities are about people helping people, and this is no different.

You won't have to worry about an explosion of SPAM on the site so long as you provide your members with acceptable outlets for self-promotion (i.e., designated discussion board areas, member profile pages—which can provide an incentive to complete those profiles, and maybe even a member showcase area) and lay out your requirements for acceptable and unacceptable forms of self-promotion in your Terms of Use. Be willing to enforce your Terms of Use with warnings and account suspensions if anyone crosses the line.

7.2. <u>Engage Your Visitors In A Conversation</u>

As discussed previously, your site visitors will want and expect a two-way exchange of information. Give them outlets for self-expression and full participation wherever possible. For example, you can provide them with any or all of the following:

- comment forms at the end of articles

- a moderated community discussion forum

- user-enabled member contact forms, which allow site members to send private messages to one another on an opt-in basis

- a sitewide contact form, allowing site visitors to easily reach you with comments, questions, issues and complaints; urge members to report abuses of the Terms of Use with this form

- Email addresses or contact forms for site contributors, allowing visitors to direct questions or feedback to article authors

You will have to decide for yourself which empowerment and communication options will work for your site without compromising its security or integrity, but do your best to empower your users as much as possible.

Even though you may be accustomed to thinking of the site as *your* site, if you build a truly successful community, your users will soon be thinking of it as *their* site—and that's a very good thing.

7.3. <u>Let Them Know You're Listening</u>

Set up autoresponders to automatically send messages back each time a visitor contacts you. This is a standard feature in CMS systems—take advantage of it.

When a user registers she should get a friendly welcome message that thanks her for taking the time to sign up, welcomes her to the community, encourages her to complete her member profile, and invites her to use the site contact form anytime she has a question, comment or issue.

Anytime a site visitor uses the contact form, he should receive a customized autoresponse keyed to the type of message he sent.

For incoming messages that require a response (i.e., bug report, question, issue, etc.), state that the message is being routed to the appropriate department or staff member and an answer will be forthcoming.

For incoming messages that don't require a response, state that the message has been received and is much appreciated, as it's feedback from site visitors that allows you to improve the site.

All contact form responses should thank the user for taking the time to send his message.

7.4. <u>Make Your Site A Village, Not A Fortress</u>

Your community will ultimately be made up of both registered members and anonymous site visitors. If you'd like to convert more of the latter into the former, draw them in by letting them see, and participate in, as much of the site as possible.

On Publetariat for example, anonymous site visitors can view all site content, use the sitewide contact form, leave comments on articles and view all areas of the discussion board. The only things they can't do, as compared to registered members, are set up a member profile page, create their own blog entries, and post to the discussion board.

While you want to hold back some premium goodies, like member profiles, member showcases, the ability to post to the discussion forum, etc. for registered users only, you also want to encourage anonymous site visitors to stick around, tell their friends about your site, come back repeatedly, and eventually, become registered members themselves.

If the majority of your content is hidden behind a "please login or register" wall, casual site visitors aren't likely to come back, nor tell their friends about the site—unless it's to warn them away from a pointless waste of time. Just as importantly, keeping your content locked away from the prying eyes of the general, websurfing public can make that content inaccessible to search engines, thereby reducing your site traffic from search engine referrals.

If you need yet another reason to let your content roam free, consider this: links to inaccessible content are links that cannot be shared on Twitter, blogs, other websites, Digg, StumbleUpon, or any other outside referrer. Your goal is to build a large, happy and engaged community, *not* a citadel of secure content.

7.5. Let Visitors Control The Content Flow

Make it as easy, flexible and convenient as possible for site visitors to stay connected to your site and content by providing an outgoing RSS feed. Don't worry about the fact that your RSS subscribers will essentially supplant your site's homepage with the RSS feed page when accessing your site, because they'll still be clicking through to the full site anytime one of the headlines in the RSS feed grabs their attention.

RSS feed page hits are still hits, and your RSS feed subscriber count is a valuable metric for measuring ongoing interest in your site. If the number starts to drop, you'll know you're not providing enough of the type of content those visitors wanted. Conversely, if you see an RSS spike following some new content initiative, you'll know that initiative is working and might want to consider expanding it.

7.6. <u>Don't Try To "Own" Your Members</u>

Your community will be just one of the many sites your members regularly visit, and *that's okay*. Nobody likes a jealous partner or controlling boss, and nobody wants to join a community that seems bent on micro-managing its users.

If your CMS allows it, make it easy for site visitors to join by embracing OpenID, a new technology that allows web users to maintain a single username and password for numerous websites. Don't worry about the fact that you don't "own" that user's registration exclusively; even if you did, what particular benefit would such exclusivity provide to you? Enabling site visitors to become members with minimal fuss, setup or demands upon them provides a strong enticement to membership.

7.7. <u>Don't Kick Your Visitors Out</u>

Wherever possible, anytime you provide links to outside sites on your site, include the target="_blank" parameter.

Standard hyperlink format is like this:

<a href="http://www.Google.com">Google</a>

When the user clicks the link, Google will load in her browser window, taking her away from your site. If she wants to return to your site after following the link but didn't bookmark it, you've just made a much bigger hassle for her to find you again.

When you include the target parameter, the link looks like this:

<a href="http://www.Google.com" target="_blank">Google</a>

When the user clicks *that* link, a new, "blank" browser window will open to load the Google page. Your site remains open in its own browser window, so when the user wants to return it's as easy as either closing the Google window or clicking back to your site's window.

In the editorial guidelines you provide to your content Contributors, be sure to state the requirement that all off-site links include the target="_blank" parameter, and spot-check the links in articles from new Contributors to be sure the parameter is in place.

.

8. A Staged Release

As site development efforts crank along, start to lay the foundation for a staged release of your community. A staged release is crucial for building site traffic early, and getting your site to go viral as quickly as possible. The stages are Pre-Launch, Beta Launch, and Go-Live.

8.1. Pre-Launch

(6 Weeks Or Less Prior To Go-Live)

You should already be fielding responses from individuals you've invited to become site contributors, and hopefully have at least a few committed to the project. Keep recruiting until you're confident you have enough contributors to keep your community frequently updated with fresh content from numerous authors.

As each new contributor is added to your roster, grant her the necessary rights and provide her with the necessary instruction to begin creating and posting content to the development site as soon as possible.

For Publetariat, I've created a Content Creation document which contains both instructions and editorial guidelines, posted it to the site server and provided each contributor with a link. When site changes or enhancements affect content creation, I update the document and send a notification to all contributors.

Encourage contributors to talk about this great new site for which they're writing on their own sites and blogs, and to leak the URL to the "coming soon" page on their sites, blogs, in Twitter posts, and so on. Ask them to encourage their own audiences to "leak" the URL on their sites and blogs, their Twitter accounts, etc. too.

What you're doing is starting a whisper campaign, in which you're raising a generalized awareness of your site among those most likely to be interested in it. You don't want to do this any sooner than about 6 weeks prior to your planned Go-Live date; any earlier, and you run the risk of people losing interest before the site is even open to the public.

Be sure to keep on top of the email address you've provided on the "coming soon" page, and either set up an autoresponder or manually respond to each visitor who writes to ask for notifications about the site. Let them know their interest is appreciated and you will be inviting them to participate in the private, Beta Launch phase.

8.2. <u>Beta Launch</u>

(3 Weeks Or Less Prior To Go-Live)

When development on your site is complete, the site has tested as fully functional, and you've got at least a little content from your contributors and/or staff in each different area of the site, it's time to press forward with your Beta Launch.

I've seen many a great-looking new site or community wither and die on the vine because the site owner didn't take a staged approach to the launch. No matter how terrific a new site looks and no matter how many great features it has, if it's like a ghost town when users show up, they'll leave and aren't likely to come back. No one wants to be first to the party, online as in real life.

The purpose of the Beta Launch is to get members registered, to get some activity going on the site, and build even more anticipation among the general public prior to your Go-Live date.

Email everyone who signed up for site notification with an invitation to the Beta Launch. In the message, make it clear that the Beta Launch is both private and exclusive, provide the direct link to the live, development site (still hidden to the general public), and invite them to register as community members. Leave the "coming soon" page in place.

Put the word out to your Contributors that the site is entering Beta Launch. Ask them to invite their respective blog or website audiences to the Beta Launch, again, providing the "secret" link to the live, development site.

Now is also the time to reach out to that other group of allies, the Influencers. Let them share news of the Beta Launch with their audiences, and get the Influencers' links up on your site if you've agreed to a link exchange agreement, but hold off on asking them to put up your ads or links until after the Go-Live.

If you get those ads and links up now, it works against you in two ways. First, it dilutes the 'secret', 'private and exclusive' effect. Second, if the ads and links reference your site's URL (as they should), anyone who follows the link at this stage will still see the "coming soon" page.

The 'secret', 'private and exclusive' aspects of the Beta Launch will make your participants feel special, as well they should, since they will be the first to experience— and hopefully, spread the news about—your terrific new community.

Depending on the duration of your Beta Launch period, you may want to solicit feedback from early site members and visitors. Don't email anyone directly, since you don't want to scare members off for fear of excessive email at this early stage. Rather, post an 'open letter from [the site]' on the site and invite visitors to use a comment form at the end of the letter to provide their feedback. If your site allows polls, you can also go with that route.

Keep monitoring your site's contact form email address (and the address provided on the "coming soon" page, if different) so you can promptly reply to any questions, invite any more interested parties to the Beta Launch, and address any problems your charter members may be having.

8.3. <u>Go-Live</u>

You should've been planning for this day before you even started building your site in earnest (see the Plan Your Launch chapter), and now it's time for the kickoff!

Take the "coming soon" page down, make sure your live site homepage is displaying correctly, and head on out to that big public event with your handouts or premiums in your hands and a great deal of enthusiasm in your heart.

8.4. <u>My Site's Go-Live</u>

Publetariat's Go-Live took place at the O'Reilly Tools of Change conference, at which I was a speaker, but there was no official announcement. The site name and URL appeared on a slide listing all the participants in the panel discussion of which I was a part, and I talked up the site and handed out cards to everyone I met. Not terribly exciting or glitzy, I know, but it provided me with the opportunity to stage a much more ambitious publicity campaign online.

I hadn't originally intended to announce Publetariat's Go-Live at the conference. Once I was there and saw the slide with Publetariat's name and URL on it however, and realized I'd probably never get a better or larger audience for the announcement, I changed my mind.

I started handing out cards and talking up the site right from the start of the conference. I'd brought the cards in anticipation of letting selected publishing industry friends and acquaintances know about Publetariat, and I ended up being very glad I'd done so.

After the conference session in which the site name and URL appeared on the session slide, I went to Twitter and posted a message that Publetariat had been 'leaked' at the conference, and since you can't stuff the genie back in the bottle, I'd have to go with it. This wasn't a completely false statement, and it definitely sparked a lot of interest in the Twitter stream. I issued an online press release using PRLog's free service as well.

Recall that for weeks in advance of the conference, a whisper campaign had kept the name of the site on the Twitter, blogosphere and web radar, so anticipation for the Go-Live announcement was high.

The TOC conference had its own, separate Twitter stream set up, and the news spread to that stream as well. Tens of thousands of people from all over the world were following the TOC stream, so the Twitter announcement actually reached a much wider audience than my on-site efforts at the conference ever could.

I posted official Go-Live announcements on my website and blogs, and asked all site Contributors, Influencers, and charter members to do the same.

Everyone who went to the site found it fully-functional, active, and community-friendly, and many of them went on to mention the site in their blogs and on their websites.

Publetariat got over 7,000 hits in its first 24 hours following the Go-Live announcement, and an Alexa traffic rating of just over 700,000 in its first week following the Go-Live announcement.

All of this was accomplished with no mainstream press coverage, no investment in marketing beyond a pack of business cards, and no time, effort or money spent on SEO. And it wasn't terribly difficult, either.

9. <u>Build On Momentum</u>

Convincing all those people to visit your new community during its launch is just the beginning. Going forward, the challenge is twofold. First, how do you keep your site visitors coming back, and second, how do you draw new visitors?

The solution to both problems is the same: keep giving site visitors and members more of the stuff that drew them in the first place.

9.1. <u>Fresh Content & Link Love</u>

Try to get new content posted on a daily basis. If your Contributors and/or staff have come up empty, scour the web for articles of interest to your audience that have been posted elsewhere for re-print on your site.

When you find a piece you'd like to re-print in its entirety, contact the author to ask for permission. Indicate that you will credit the article to the author and provide a link back to the site on which the piece originally appeared (a.k.a., you will give the author/site 'link love'). If the author has a separate site or blog, also offer to include a link to that site or blog.

Everyone's looking for more site traffic; if you've already established your community as a site to be reckoned with in terms of traffic, authors of those articles you want will be only too happy to be featured so prominently on your site. Encourage them to publicize the reprinted piece on their sites, blogs, via Twitter, etc. and it becomes a real win-win-win situation.

In one fell swoop you've given your audience what *they* want (fresh content), the author what *he* wants (exposure to a new audience), and you've gotten what *you* want (happy community members and new visitors).

If you can't find any contact information for the author, or don't have time to wait for a response, re-print an excerpt of the desired piece. Excerpt no more than 50% of the piece, and err on the side of less. Reprint just enough to pique the reader's interest, so he'll want to read the rest.

Precede the excerpt with an Editor's Note indicating who wrote the piece, where it originally appeared (with an embedded link back to that site), and the date on which it originally appeared. At the end of the excerpt, print a "continue reading this article at [site name]" message, again, with an embedded link back to that site.

Just as with pieces reprinted in their entirety, if the author has a separate site or blog, also include a link to that site or blog (i.e., "You can learn more about [author name] and his work at [author's site or blog].").

In a case where you can't reach the author of the excerpted article you can't expect to get exposure for your site on her site, but it's still a win-win. The author gets exposure on your site and your audience gets fresh content and a warm, fuzzy impression of your site's generosity with the link love. You're giving them yet another reason to view your site as a homey, welcoming and friendly place, rather than a corporate sales front.

Don't forget to set the "target" parameter of your links to "_blank", so that the other site will open in a new window and your site will remain open in its own window.

9.2. <u>Keep The Lines of Communication Open</u>

Remember that contact form you built into your site? You *have* been checking for messages daily and responding to them promptly, right?

Most CMS systems provide a polling module. If yours does, use it! How better to get a bead on what your audience is thinking? But don't use polls for that purpose alone, also employ them as fun diversions for your audience.

9.3. <u>Don't Get Complacent</u>

No matter how great your site traffic is trending, try to maintain the same underdog, new-guy-on-the-block attitude and work ethic with which you began. Complacency is the enemy.

Your outside Contributors are not likely to stay with you forever, nor are the Influencers with whom you've exchanged links. Keep up the effort to recruit new Contributors and Influencers, and maintain a list of likely future candidates. That way, when the flow of new content and new visitors from outside sites slows down, you're ready to act.

Frequently peruse your members' comments, blog entries and discussion board posts so you can quickly respond to any issues, problems or feature wish-lists that are being discussed on the site but not submitted on your site contact form.

Keeping your finger on the pulse of your community will also help you to anticipate their needs *before* they need to ask. For example, if you see a lot of chatter about a single topic in the catch-all, off-topic discussion board area, you may want to create a new discussion board area for site members to discuss that topic in a dedicated location.

10. Monetizing

The second you or your bosses decide your site traffic has reached critical mass, the question of monetization will arise: how can you make the site self-supporting, or even profitable?

Tread lightly and with great caution, because this is another one of those critical junctures where a wrong move can undo a great deal of your effort and accumulated goodwill among community members. A *serious* gaffe can even sink your site entirely.

10.1. Advertising

You've built up your community's loyalty and trust by empowering them, keeping a two-way conversation going, and being responsive to their needs. You've given them an online home away from home, and made them feel comfortable there. So far, so good.

Now, how do people react when a large, hard-sell billboard goes up near their homes? Do they welcome flashing neon outside their bedroom windows? And how do they feel about telemarketing calls, junk mail, junk fax and SPAM? Hate it, hate it, and hate it, right? So you can imagine how they'll react if one day, they come to their online home away from home to find it's become annoyingly cluttered with excessive advertising messages.

Your community has come to expect a certain amount of advertising online, but that doesn't mean you can keep piling up the ads until someone complains. By that time, visitors will already be leaving in numbers; it's too late .

Make every effort to keep the advertising on your site targeted to the interests and needs of your community, and don't allow the quantity or type of advertising to compete with site content.

10.2. Premium Membership

Offering a paid, premium level of membership is another monetization option. Premium-level members can receive benefits such as blog upgrades (i.e., additional template and theme options, greater formatting control, blog widgets, etc.), enhanced member profile pages, and a private chat room, for example.

Avoid making content access conditional on paid membership, however; remember, you want your community to be like a village, not a fortress.

10.3. Merchandise

Depending on the thing around which your community was built, site-branded merchandise can provide another revenue stream. It's a safe bet if either the thing around which the community was built or the community itself has a high degree of kitsch-appeal or cool among members of the general public.

Likewise, if your community members have become very loyal to your site and have come to feel a sense of pride in association with it, it's very likely they'll want to own t-shirts, coffee mugs, tote bags, mousepads and other merchandise that reflects that association.

10.4. Selling Your Own Goods Or Services

If your community is a corporate-backed initiative, it's likely that the opportunity to sell goods or services was the entire reason why your community was launched in the first place. You *can* do it, but it's easy to turn your audience off in the process.

Look at selling goods and services to your community the same way you would look at selling to friends and family. Like friends and family, your community will expect to be treated a little better than the general public. Offer them price breaks, premium versions of your product or service, and other perks.

For example, a community built around books might be offered signed editions of a given book when they pre-order the book. Another, built around software, can be offered a free extension on the tech support that comes standard with software purchase.

10.5. How To Get It Wrong

Choose your strategic partnerships carefully and plan their rollout with just as much care, lest your audience be left with the impression that you've been operating with a hidden agenda all along. Consider the following, cautionary tale.

A new online community was born one day, with the stated purpose of allowing writers to workshop their manuscripts there. Following periods of peer review, the top-rated manuscripts would be brought to the attention of mainstream publishers.

The community grew and thrived, generating much loyalty and goodwill among its membership, and after many months, a few member manuscripts were indeed put under contract with publishers.

Understandably, there was much disappointment and gnashing of teeth among those members whose manuscripts were not chosen for publication, but the cycles of peer review continued and the slim odds of selling a manuscript for publication were generally accepted by the community.

One day, the site announced a strategic alliance with a self-publishing outfit and framed it as a service they would be offering to their valued membership. I can't say what the true motivation behind the alliance was: offering a much-needed service to meet the needs of its membership, or setting up a new revenue stream built on a percentage of each self-publishing deal struck. But I *can* tell you the rollout backfired.

In minutes, the community discussion forums were ablaze with angry posts from members who assumed a profit motive and felt completely betrayed by the site they'd come to trust. In addition to the objection to being sold, en masse, a service in which they'd expressed no interest, they also took offense at the implication that most members' manuscripts had no hope of mainstream publication.

In the hours and days that followed, many in the community not only cancelled their memberships but went on to badmouth the site on their blogs, websites, Twitter and the like. Contrary to popular opinion, not *all* publicity is *good* publicity.

The people running the site could have foreseen this outcome if they'd been paying attention to their membership. In the discussion area of the site, members had previously been exchanging their thoughts about self-publication and the majority of opinion was steadfastly negative.

In spite of the vocal majority's anti-self-publish sentiment, the site runners still could've pulled off the alliance rollout without alienating anyone. They could have done any of the following:

- Reach out to Influencers from online, self-publishing communities to bring in more pro-self-publishing site visitors ahead of the rollout

- Soften up the group ahead of time by posting some self-publish success stories or interviews with self-published authors on the site

- Post a series of articles about various publishing options well in advance of the rollout, therein presenting self-publishing as a legitimate option

- Keep the rollout low-key, couched in terms like, "We've noticed that some of our members are interested in self-publishing, and as a service to those members we have formed an alliance with [company name] to bring you..."

Bottom line: if you intend to form any strategic alliances with providers of goods or services, think long and hard about how those alliances may be perceived by your community first; then proceed very carefully.

11. Conclusion

The single, guiding principle behind building successful communities, whether online or in the real world, is this:

Communities are about *people*, not *things*.

You may think you're building a book, car, wildlife conservation or anime community, but you're wrong. You're building a community of *people* who happen to share an interest in books, cars, wildlife conservation or anime.

Nobody wants to be a member of the Proctor & Gamble club, with the possible exception of P&G employees, but plenty would want to get involved in a community that can provide them with tips for simplifying and economizing housekeeping chores. Similarly, no one among the general public wants to belong to a General Motors community, but there are plenty who'd gladly join a community for Silverado truck owners.

The difference is that a P&G or GM club puts the brand ahead of the people, whereas a housekeeping or Silverado community puts the interests of the people ahead of the brand.

Keep the focus on the interests of the people in your community, and you'll rarely go wrong. And when something seems to be amiss in your community, it's a safe bet you've taken your eye off the "interests of the people" ball.

About the Author

April L. Hamilton is an author, blogger, Technorati BlogCritic, leading advocate for the indie author movement and the founder of Publetariat.com. In her popular self-published reference book, The Indie Author Guide, she offers aspiring self-published authors a roadmap to publishing success. She is also the author of novels available in both ebook and POD form. As a former software engineer and web developer, April enjoys immersing herself in ebook, Print on Demand and other emerging publishing technologies for self-published authors.

April lives in Southern California with her husband, two children, and entirely too many pets.

http://www.publetariat.com
http://www.aprillhamilton.com
http://aprillhamilton.blogspot.com

www.ingramcontent.com/pod-product-compliance
Lightning Source LLC
Chambersburg PA
CBHW071252170526
45165CB00003B/1319